Eugene A. Walsh

Proclaiming God's Love

IN SONG

Foreword by Elaine Rendler

OCP Publications

We of OCP Publications thank
Ruth Eger
Fred J. Nijem and
Elaine Rendler
who helped prepare this work
in memory of their dear friend
Gene Walsh

Excerpts from *Music in Catholic Worship,* © 1983, USCC; *Liturgical Music Today,* © 1982, USCC are used by license of the copyright owner. All rights reserved.

Cover design: Ralph Sanders

Contents

Foreword

There are many facets to Eugene Walsh. Eugene A. Walsh, S.S., the *academic,* was a solid theologian, a seminary professor, music director and a wise and educated man. Father Gene, the *priest,* was a life-giving presider, compassionate confessor and, most of all, passionate preacher and proclaimer of the good news. He proclaimed God's love both in word and in song. Within these contexts Gene was a colorful teacher who influenced several generations of ministers called by ordination or baptism or both.

Although he was always more than willing to take credit where credit was due, he never claimed to have all the answers. Opinionated, yes . . . but he never aspired to be the omega point. For many of us Gene was just the opposite: He was the starting point. He had the ability to break open complex theological-liturgical concepts so that everybody could understand. He knew how to cut through the babble to get to the essence of what needed to be said and done.

Gene wrote this book to get people started in the ministry of music. It is almost unchanged from the original so as to keep his style intact. Hopefully, this brief encounter with the insight and knowledge of Gene will get you started. Perhaps you will be replenished by his spirit. He planted seeds that have yielded a harvest of competent priests, pastoral musicians and liturgical ministers. May *Proclaiming God's Love in Song* send you on your way.

— Elaine Rendler, D.M.A.

What Music Taught Me

For years I directed choirs at the seminary and cathedral in Baltimore. When I began in the early forties, the theme, "God's presence," echoed through the writings of our spiritual leaders. Those leaders helped us ask, "How can we keep God constantly before us throughout the work day?" What a big question! What a big achievement — if we could pull it off. These writers offered assorted techniques to help us make it work. Some even guaranteed their methods. It all grew complicated and called for tricky spiritual acrobatics.

From the very start, that approach caused me no little problem in working with choirs. My problem was simple. How could I give all my attention to doing my work with the choir and at the same time keep a door open for remaining in God's presence? It frustrated me. If I got in God's corner, I lost hold of the choir. And if I paid attention to the choir, I forgot about God. I had a dilemma that stayed with me for years. I felt divided. So I got some help.

Then I also got some sense. I realized finally that

I couldn't play the division game any longer. I could not give my full attention to the choir's needs and to God's presence at the same time. So I stopped trying and started doing one thing at a time.

I gave all my attention to the choir during rehearsal. I devoted myself entirely to God during prayer. I opened my doors wide to nature, to art, to music, to people and to the Holy Spirit. It worked for me.

OPENNESS TO CREATION

We grow to adulthood by opening ourselves to creation and to people. In fact, it's the only way. Nothing substitutes for it. Without initial openness, there will be no beginnings, middles or endings. Closed people don't grow. They remain children throughout their adult life. This comes as no surprise. At times it seems that child adults even outnumber grown-up adults. We need to take a closer look at the correlation between openness and growth.

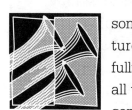 I find openness the key — openness to different personalities, diversity in culture, variety of experience, nature, the earth, the world, all creation. We grow to fullness as persons when we realize, insofar as we can, all the gifts God gives us. We realize this potential by connecting to all that is inside us and outside us. We relate to God, ourselves, neighbors, creation, ideas, arts, science, history. If we do not connect and relate, we shrivel up and die. We grow by relating. (See *Spirituality: Christian Life in the World Today,* by Eugene A. Walsh, pages 18–48.)

OPENNESS TO THE SPIRIT

Openness to creation leads us to the Spirit of Christ. Life in the world can open us to life in faith: to the life we sum up in the word *spirituality.* The basic rule is simple. We open ourselves to the Spirit of Christ when we open ourselves to the world and to people. The Spirit comes to us through the world in which we live and through the people with whom we relate. The Spirit already works in the world and in us, seeking to be released into our lives, into others' lives and into all creation. That is what we mean when we pray to the Holy Spirit, "Renew the face of the earth."

We have priorities in living according to the Spirit who renews the earth. The top priority is this: We make ourselves as open as we can in every way we can. To do that, we have to find out just how open we are. It's not easy. We cannot always get an accurate reading by ourselves. We may need others to let us know how they see us. That may be hard and may take a lot of courage. How does our family see us? The neighbors? Colleagues? Anything we can discover about ourselves in this way will be of great value.

Where do we stand on the scale that extends from closed to open? If we get an accurate reading on how open we are, we can do something about it, should we choose. If we never find out, we remain slaves of ignorance and captives of fantasy. We stay closed. I find particularly tragic on the human stage the great number of people who close themselves to change and don't know it.

A genuine, life-giving freedom in the Spirit comes about as we consciously open ourselves to the circumstances of our lives, especially to the people around us. If we go

I find openness the key — openness to different personalities, diversity in culture, variety of experience, nature, the earth, the world, all creation.

 off in another direction, we wind up doing unproductive or even destructive things.

We describe here an important principle of Christian life: we open doors that keep us from each other and break down barriers that alienate us from creation. We open ourselves to the Spirit. There is no other way. If we close ourselves to the world in which we live and to the people with whom we live, we close ourselves to God. In other words, we grow in the life of faith to the degree that we work with the Holy Spirit to "renew the face of the earth."

INVOLVEMENT AND EXCELLENCE

Another principle of Christian life flows from this openness: we live life as thoroughly as we can. We get involved. We do well what we do — at whatever time.

- We involve ourselves in each value for its own sake. That's our best reason for doing anything: because it is worthwhile in itself. We respect every part of creation because it deserves our respect. We love people for their own sake, not for God's sake. If we love people primarily for *God's* sake, we insult them. Are they not lovable in themselves? We seek them out, pay them attention, respect them, love them, because they have their own worth and beauty.

- We involve ourselves actively in the business of loving ourselves. We seek to love ourselves more and more, because we are lovable. God made us that way: lovable. We deserve all the love we give ourselves. Failure to love ourselves insults the God who created us. Guilt — imposed by others and increased by us — constitutes the greatest barrier to love of self and love of God. Guilt results from human weakness and sin. God has nothing to do with it. We need to break through the guilt barrier in loving ourselves enough to open up to the Spirit.

- We involve ourselves in our work, job, study or time off. We do this in every possible way. We put ourselves into whatever we do. We give it all our energy. We don't hold back. When we immerse ourselves in a task, we move closer to the Spirit of God. Is not that the goal? Also, by the same wholehearted attention, we turn out a more excellent work. In the process, we do not need to be aware of God at all. All we need is to be involved as completely as possible.

We grow in the life of faith to the degree that we work with the Holy Spirit to "renew the face of the earth."

Total involvement lays the foundation. If we skip this step, how will God provide the growth, the increase, the fruit? To involve ourselves less than completely is to put a coating of sugar on our cereal. It may taste all right for awhile, but it bores us quickly. Our enthusiasm wanes. The momentum collapses.

Such built-in failure characterizes the programs of many "schools of spirituality." They fail through superficiality. Their programs fail because they come from outside the self. They grow routine, mechanical, boring. We do not invest much in them. As a result, we end up worse off than when we began. And we blame the failure on ourselves rather than on the "school." The "school" with its programs is the real culprit. Now we need to learn from the big mistake.

LIVING IN THE PRESENCE OF GOD

A final principle of Christian life could take this form: we do not take responsibility for God's loving presence. This insight runs

 counter to some prevailing notions of spirituality. In the good old days, what counted was our intention or our good will. Now we are saying that thorough involvement in our task is even more important. Our desire to do the most excellent job we can counts most. We don't even have to be conscious of God in the process. And that may need further explanation.

- God is always close to us. It's a simple fact. God makes promises of faithful love and keeps those promises. God's business is to draw near. Nothing we do can change that. Nor does our consciousness or lack of consciousness of God's presence make it more or less so. A sense of God's loving closeness feels good. Such feelings affirm and help us. God offers them at important times. But they really do not provide the only evidence of God's closeness to us. God is always there, even when we don't have warm feelings.

- We frustrate ourselves by trying to accomplish two important things at the same time: an awareness of God's presence and a job well done. We can't divide our mind or our heart. And if our job has importance and requires care, do we have a right to give it less? To do a mediocre job is to betray God's purpose.

Pierre Teilhard de Chardin helps us understand this. Through his writings, a refreshing theme echoes: by giving ourselves totally to the task, we surrender to God directly and immediately.

PERSONAL REFLECTIONS

Reading Teilhard de Chardin was a high point in my life. What a moment of conversion God gave! With dazzling clarity I realized God's closeness to us — and our nearness to God, even when we don't think about it or feel it. This was a great moment, a powerful insight, a wonderful discovery.

As a result, I started to live with an abiding sense of God's and our presence to each other — precisely in our work. I didn't have to be thinking about it all the time. What a relief! No more acrobatics!

I got excited about the insight and shared it with others. With this awareness came another discernment, no less worthy. It concerns liturgical music.

By giving our undivided attention to music, we enable the assembly to tap into the full power and life-giving energy that flows from making beautiful music together. The gift we offer members of the assembly through music is encouragement to open themselves to the work of the Spirit at that moment. Music helps the great symbols come to life: gathering, reconciling, responding, proclaiming, acclaiming, petitioning, remembering, thanking, praising, celebrating, sending forth. Music helps open our hearts to become receptive or vulnerable to the Spirit's work.

Now I look back with delight, knowing that the music we made all those years performed a needed service for God's people. For some it occasioned conversion. To others it gave comfort and reassurance. Still others it drew more fully into the celebration.

Those of us who did the hard and happy work of ministering music received something else: a deep, lasting satisfaction. We all knew that we were doing something good. That realization prompted efforts to do even better. Liturgical ministers, includ-

God is always close to us. It's a simple fact. God makes promises of faithful love and keeps those promises. God's business is to draw near.

13

ing musicians, need to derive regular satisfaction from our work. If we don't, we burn out and quit. We give up and start the restless search for something else. But why look further? What we seek is right here.

We rejoiced mightily in our work. How wonderful! We knew what we were doing, understood why, enjoyed it and took pleasure in our enjoyment. We suspected that it pleased and delighted God a great deal too.

The Bigger Picture of the Parish Sunday Assembly

Where Music Ministers Fit

In order to translate our vision of the parish church into a truly life-giving celebration of Sunday eucharist — to experience genuine ritual rather than lifeless rubrics — we must constantly remember several points. First, we must recall that the desired outcome of our Sunday liturgy is not a head-trip, but conversion. The purpose of a Sunday eucharist celebration is to help make possible some form of encounter with the living Jesus who is present in this sacramental action. In the celebration, members of the assembly need to experience Christ's saving action in such a way that it transforms them into the image of God.

Second, we need to realize that sacraments are not things, but the personal actions of all those who celebrate. We can no longer think in terms of "giving and receiving sacraments." All members of the assembly give the sacraments. All receive the sacraments. And all celebrate the sacraments.

Third, we must remember that liturgical ministers are not better than, holier than, or higher than the rest of the assembly. Genuine ministry is best described in terms of personal presence, service and competence. Let's look a bit closer at each of these three qualities.

- *Personal Presence.* The deliberate, intended, personal presence of all ministers is the energy that, in the Spirit, makes sacraments life-giving.

- *Service.* Genuine ministry is always a matter of service, never a matter of status. Ministry is helping others exercise their own ministries.

- *Competence.* Competent ministers are willing to do their homework, to work with others, to develop skills and to practice. The slogan or motto for all ministry could go something like this: Put yourself into it. Work with the team. Do it with a touch of class. Above all, enjoy it!

Fourth, we need to respect the nature and demands of ritual actions. We *discover* ritual and enter into it. We do not make up ritual. In submitting to the discipline of ritual, we deliberately take on the roles that are demanded by the ritual action. We play these roles as best we can. For instance, members of the assembly deliberately transform themselves from mere individuals into gatherers, public prayers, singers, storytellers, music makers, dancers, readers, presiders, listeners, and so forth. Above all, ritual makers work as a team.

Fifth, we must keep in mind that storytelling and symbol making are the two great energies that generate the powerful images of ritual action. In all the activity of celebrating Sunday eucharist, particularly in the liturgy of the word and in the liturgy of the eucharist, we work to tell our story as a people and to celebrate our story in life-giving symbols.

- *Story.* Every member of the assembly should be helped to know the story, to retell the story, and to recognize how the seasonal and Sunday proclamation of the scripture fits into the story.

- *Symbols.* In order to make life-giving symbols, we need to distinguish between those symbols that are essential in a life-giving celebration from the many other less important symbols. The primary symbol of the eucharist is the *assembly* in all its celebrating activity (gathering, praying, singing, proclaiming God's word and listening, taking part in in the Lord's supper).

Sixth, we must respect the basic structure of the Sunday eucharist. At the present time, Sunday eucharist has two main parts (the liturgy of the word and the liturgy of the eucharist) and three lesser parts (entrance rite, preparation of the gifts, and dismissal rite). In celebrating, the idea is to make the main parts appear as main parts and not to let the lesser parts overwhelm them. At times the entrance rite is so piled high with song and word that it appears more important than the liturgy of the word. The same can happen with the preparation of the gifts. This is poor ritual.

Gathering expresses a horizontal energy that engages the members of the assembly in a mutual sharing that tends to make them feel at ease.

Seventh, we must remember that good liturgy is good drama. In order to be life-giving, good liturgy has to have a dynamic pattern. This dynamic pattern consists of ebb and flow, tension and release. The assembly must enter into three actions — gathering, listening, responding — to make the drama take place. Gathering is the topic of this chapter. Listening is the topic of chapter three. Responding is the topic of chapter four. Like a ballet, the rhythm of good ritual action begins, gathers momentum and moves relentlessly to a climax. Each part of the action has its own inner dynamic. All the parts fit together to make a single unified action. Careful choreography rules out all that is irrelevant to the rite; it makes the action flow smoothly and freely. The same care in designing the movement of the ritual secures a rise in tension and then a release. We can portray this design in the following way:

- *Gathering.* This action expresses a horizontal energy that engages the members of the assembly in a mutual sharing that tends to make them feel at ease.
- *Listening.* The liturgy of the word demands a deliberate tension. Members of the assembly are called upon to give wholehearted and undivided attention in receiving the word and in responding to the word.
- *Responding.* The eucharistic prayer calls for the active paraticipation of members of the assembly. The eucharistic prayer leads directly to the communion rite, in which the members of the assembly bond and seal their declared unity by sharing the common plate and the common cup. The dismissal moves the assembly to the conclusion of Sunday eucharist and to the assembly's ministry in daily life.

Eighth, we need to remember to pay careful attention *ahead of time* to the fundamentals of our worship environment. Fundamentals, such as the following, will help make the celebration life-giving.

- *Light.* People respond strongly and unconsciously to light and darkness. We have no power to change this fact. We do, however, have the power to make light work for us rather than against us. Because light engenders life and energy, light is an important help in encouraging hospitality. Semidarkness is a liability.
- *Sound.* Sound has a profound effect on people. It can nurture or destroy. Unpleasant electronic sound has much power to turn people off. Pleasant sound, on the other hand, tends to draw people into the word that is being proclaimed and the music that is played or sung. A good sound system is essential to good worship.

- *Space.* Cluttered space is inhospitable space. It acts like a "don't walk on the grass" sign. It tells people they are not welcome. In contrast, uncluttered space is inviting. It tells people they are welcome. After the important spaces for Sunday celebration have been clearly identified and beautifully established, we need to remove all unnecessary articles of furniture: extra chairs, kneelers, candles. However, such removal should always be sensitive to the needs of the assembly. Replacement or movement of familiar furniture must be preceded by careful public explanation of the reason for the change.

1. Assembly Space. The foremost space in the church is the space of the assembly. Effective entry space helps people to gather. Effective us of assembly space allows people to see one another without great effort.

2. Other Spaces: (altar, lectern, presider's chair, vestibule). The arrangement of each of these spaces guarantees that the minister who leads will be easily visible to the members of the assembly. These different spaces are clearly identified, functional, not crowding each other and not in competition with each other.

3. Music Space. The space for music ministers should be located in a way that allows them to carry out both their role as leaders of the assembly and as participants in the prayer and worship. Ordinarily this space is up front and to the side. Choir galleries do not work. The song leader is visible enough for easy communication with the assembly.

 Last but not least, we need to have a parish liturgical policy that spells out the normal pattern of celebration in the parish and the reasons for each detail in the pattern, particularly when such details differ from inherited assumptions. The considerations sketched briefly in the preceding pages — along with the ritual patterns that

follow — can offer a basis for a genuine policy in your parish for celebrating Sunday eucharist. These suggestions and principles will become policy when they are formally adopted as the norms by which Sunday eucharist in the parish is discussed, preached, prepared and celebrated.

The Assembly as Minister

In order to develop an effective gathering rite — rite of hospitality — there are some points we must have always in mind. Before proceeding, let's recall them: 1) Gathering is an essential ritual for making a life-giving church. 2) Gathering is a ministry. It is the first ministry of the entire assembly. 3) Gathering takes place when members of the assembly take the trouble to come together with one other. They come to church to share themselves with each other and to exercise the ministry of hospitality. 4) Gathering in God's name is "church." The church is people gathered.

The gathering rite is a single action that starts at home and moves to the liturgy of the word. The action of the gathering rite can be divided into three parts: the gathering process, a preparation period, and the entrance rite.

THE GATHERING PROCESS

The gathering process is a living and life-giving symbol of hospitality. The message is clear: "You are welcome. We want you to be at home here. We cherish you and care about you." Deliberate and gracious effort at hospitality is the first and indispensable step on the way to genuine Christian love. It is the first movement in fulfilling God's commandment to love each other. Don't talk about loving each other or pretend to do so if you are not willing to say hello.

Gracious hospitality generates a form of healing no one can

ever truly estimate. We will never know how much it means to a person, beaten down by all kinds of distress, to have someone take the trouble to smile and express caring. If we are really serious about healing of any kind, this is where to start.

I suggest recruiting people for key roles in this gathering ministry be carried out in as personal a manner as possible. Take the time to explain clearly *why* the process is so important.

We will never know how much it means to a person, beaten down by all kinds of distress, to have someone take the trouble to smile and express caring.

In the process of parish conversion, the church is engaged in an operation that calls for revolutionary change of behavior on the part of most church-going Catholics. For centuries most Catholics have been coming to church with the expectation that others will "do the Mass" for them. Suddenly they are called to change patterns of behavior that are part of their long heritage. They need lots of help and a good period of time to make the transition.

There will always be those members of the parish who do not respond. They can't respond, or they won't. The reasons make no difference. These people are members of the parish and have a perfect right to be there. A parish that is pastorally sensitive will always make room for them, pay attention to them, cherish them. Parish ministers who have sensitivity will not nag these people or try to bully them into activity that they are unwilling or unable to accept.

A worthwhile enhancement of this basic program would be to stage a "name tag Sunday" once a month. On this day, all parishioners wear name tags and make even a greater effort to be hospitable.

I would also like to urge that the bringing of generous quantities of food for distribution to the needy become an expected part of the Sunday gathering ritual in every parish — especially if there is so much food that it clutters up the place! A significant gathering of food for the needy is a vital symbol as well as a genuine response of people as church. In any event, the food goods should make a pile that can be seen easily by everyone at some time or other. (If the parish does not run its own food bank, the people should be made aware of the churches or agencies that will distribute the food.) What is important is that this gathering of food become expected, familiar and repeated ritual behavior.

The eventual goal at this point in the order of the Mass is that *all* (or as many as possible) members of the parish will come to Mass on Sunday with the deliberate intention of taking part in the gathering rite. Throughout the program, all members of the assembly are encouraged to make it their first business, once they are seated, to speak to those around them, both sides, front and back.  The hope is that this will become, through time and familiarity, "second nature" for assembly members, as silence once was and still is.

Within the gathering process we can identify three phases or stages: the ministry of the members of the assembly, the ministry of ushers, greeters, hosts, and the ministry of presiders, deacons and others. Let us explore these stages separately.

Stage One: Ministry of the Members of the Assembly.

To begin, select one of the more popular Masses. Enlist the help of two or three couples who are not otherwise involved in church ministry. Ask these couples to do some serious phone-calling for a reasonable time. (These couples would work at this for about six months, at which time other couples would take over.)

The phone calls: The two or three couples should call about thirty different people who regularly attend the selected Mass. The goal here is to get a mixture of families, individuals, single parents, brothers, sisters. Describe the following ministry for them. Ask them to take part in it and to commit for at least six months.

The ministry: Come to Mass fifteen or twenty minutes ahead of time. Weather permitting, park your car and wait with your family in the parking lot until another car comes alongside or nearby. Introduce yourselves to the other people and find out who they are. Chat with them as you go together into church and encourage them to sit with you. When you get seated, continue to find out about these people. Also turn to the front and back of you and greet the people who are there. Ask their names and tell them you are glad to see them.

Stage Two: Ministry of Ushers, Greeters, Hosts.

At life-giving celebrations, greeters are stationed at each door with their name written large on name tags. Their task is to greet and welcome all who enter. Most of all, greeters are to look for and try to identify new parishioners and visitors. Behind the greeters in the entrance foyer, a select number of people are waiting. They will act as hosts and hostesses during Mass for those new people who are discovered by the greeters. The hosts and hostesses take their visitors to prime seats, help them find any needed worship aids, introduce them to people nearby and tell them something of the parish story. They invite their guests to whatever function the parish may offer after Mass.

Stage Three: Ministry of Presiders, Deacons.

The presider, deacons and other ministers who can be available, make it a priority to be free in order to mingle with the people *inside* the church, paying particular heed to those who call for some special attention (for instance, a recent death in the family, a new baby, a return from the hospital, etc.). In sharing this kind of hospitality, the presider and the ministers are quietly assuring many other people that it is quite all right and desirable to talk in church.

Music ministers do well to participate in this hospitality for at least a few minutes prior to the preparation period introduced by the presider. This means taking care of rehearsals, warm-ups and music organizing a few minutes earlier than is typical. Bright, inviting prelude music can also contribute much to the hospitable atmosphere we are trying to create. People feel more free to speak with each other if there's music in the air.

THE PREPARATION PERIOD

If we are serious about helping members of the parish assembly accept deliberate, active participation as their important and expected ministry, we must have some sort of preparation period at the beginning of Sunday eucharist. It is important to regard such a preparation period as a regular part of the celebration and not just as rehearsal time.

The preparation period serves a number of important purposes. First, it provides a steady and persistent way for letting assembly members know that what they do at Mass is important and the celebration can't do without it. Furthermore, it says very clearly that assembly members have a need to prepare for their ministry just as all other ministers do. Any other approach seems to say to the members of the assembly: "What you do at Mass is really not very important and we can get along quite well without you, thank you."

Second, the preparation period serves a more immediate purpose of "breaking the ice." Whenever people gather, they need to be brought to a point of focus to perform the tasks they are supposed to do. It is really absurd to expect people who have no history of responding in prayer and song to do so automatically and without some form of preparation. Without this short preparation period, I am quite sure we will never succeed in helping to bring the assembly to awareness that a life-giving celebration of Sunday eucharist depends on their deliberate and active participation.

The preparation period needs strict monitoring. It lasts no more than five minutes, ever. If it is kept carefully within this time limit, people will accept the preparation period as a regular part of getting ready for celebrating Mass.

A well-designed and effective preparation can be set up in this way: 1) At a designated time (five minutes before Mass time or exactly at Mass time), the presider goes to the front of the church and greets people in this way: "Good morning. (Good afternoon.) We gather again to help each other pray and to worship God together." 2) The presider then asks for a response to dialogue

 prayer: "The Lord be with you." Regardless of how the assembly's first response comes through, he asks for a more energetic and wholehearted response a second time around. By means of this simple effort, he helps the assembly move from uncertainty and shyness to a full response. From this experience people gain the confidence. 3) The presider remains where he is but yields to the music leader. The presider gives his own attention to that person helping the assembly with a new response or song. The presider's presence is an important support for the music person. 4) When introducing new music, it is important that the music leader precede it with a brief review of something very familiar. This gives people an initial experience of how well they can sing. 5) In teaching new music, the music leader should remember that it does not

help at all to urge people with verbal pleas to participate. Such an approach turns quickly to nagging. 6) After about four minutes of music practice, the presider gets ready for the ritual beginning of Mass, however it has been arranged. Use this preparation period carefully for a year as outlined above, and I guarantee that you will see a remarkable transformation in the parish assembly!

THE ENTRANCE RITE

The entrance rite should be seen not as the first part of liturgy but as the last part of the gathering rite. All that has gone before in the gathering rite is properly liturgy. Liturgy begins long before ritual. A formal entrance rite, however, serves as the *ritual* beginning of the celebration.

The entrance rite does not exist for its own sake. It is entirely introductory. Its total energy is to bring us to something else. The real purpose of the entrance rite is to make a formal beginning of ritual prayer and song and to lead us immediately to the liturgy of the word. Thus the entrance rite achieves its sign value best of all when it is brief and leads directly to its goal. When the rite gets overstuffed, it bogs down and fails miserably to achieve its purpose.

Liturgists are in general agreement that the entrance rite is still somewhat cluttered. The rite, in its present form, consists of a call to worship, the gathering song (with procession or alternate form), a greeting (with very brief statement of the day's theme by the presider), the penitential rite (in whatever form), the Glory to God, and the prayer of the assembly. The major parts are song, greeting and prayer. These should be highlighted. The peniten-

The entrance rite does not exist for its own sake. . . . Its total energy is to bring us to something else.

tial rite and the Glory to God are of secondary importance. Neither should be given too much prominence.

The entrance rite is one of several places in the liturgy where great care and discipline must be used to avoid "verbal overkill." Ministers should take care that the statement of the theme or the petitions of the penitential rite do not become wordy, rambling discourse. Short sentences and simple words are the best.

I believe the motto for all entrance rites should be, "Get me to the word on time . . . and with lots of energy!"

I also suggest that you do not use "canned" material. I urge you to use your own words. They are much more likely to be listened to. Aim to say what you want in the *fewest* words and with as many words of Anglo-Saxon origin as possible. Anglo-Saxon words communicate much more powerfully than do words of Latin origin. Try it and see how well it works!

Many parishes lead off their entrance rite with a rather lengthy statement of theme. Often this statement is a sort of mini-homily. After a lot of observing and reflection, I suggest that this is pretty much a waste of time. It is the beginning of verbal overkill.

Instead, I find it advisable to reserve any statement of theme to the presider's introduction after his greeting, as part of his introduction to the penitential rite. The reasons are compelling. First, there should be only one such introduction, if any at all. Second, such introduction is part of the presider's role as leader of the eucharistic celebration. Third, such an introduction, carefully nuanced and live, gives the presider the opportunity to enter personally into the celebration and to make connections with the other members of the assembly. Fourth, the people are inclined to listen to the presider if he does it live and doesn't just read something in mechanical fashion. Fifth, this is a fine opportunity to cut out some of the word-fat that so plagues our Sunday worship.

In short, I believe the motto for all entrance rites should be, "Get me to the word on time . . . and with lots of *energy!*" Having said this, I would now like to discuss the parts of the entrance rite in detail. An effective entrance rite could be set up in the following way:

Call to Worship. The call to worship should be made from some place other than the lectern. (The lectern should be reserved for the reading of scripture only.) The stand of the song leader is a proper place from which to make this announcement. The call to worship should be made by someone other than the reader. (The reader's ministry should be reserved only for the proclamation of the word.) The song leader or one of the music ministers would do very well.

When it is time to begin, the community leader or the song leader calls the community to worship. He or she invites the people to stand and join in the opening song. A formula something like the following serves very well:

> *"Welcome to the 10:00 o'clock Mass at St. Ann's.*
> *Welcome particularly to our new parishioners and our*
> *visitors. My name is Mary O'Dea. Our presider is*
> *Father Tom Smith. Please stand and sing our*
> *gathering song: Number 48, "O God, Our Help In*
> *Ages Past."*

It is not proper to say: "Please stand and greet our presider with our opening song." That is not the purpose of the song at all. The opening song is a gathering song for the entire assembly, not a welcoming song for the presider.

It is possible to include in the opening statement the names of other ministers (lector, eucharistic ministers), unless the list is too long. If there are too many names to call out, include them in the bulletin. People get bored with long lists. In this situation less is always better than more.

I respectfully suggest that the call to worship is *not* an appropriate place to read any verbal statement of "theme." It is a waste of time here, for people do not really listen. If there is to be any such statement, the presider can do it very briefly in his own carefully chosen words, using the pattern explained below.

Gathering Song With Procession. The gathering song, not the procession, is the important part of this rite. The song is the assembly's first ritual action of prayer and praise. The music and words should be of such substance that the assembly can recognize and claim them as their own. Furthermore, the song should be appropriate to the occasion — a song of praise, blessing, or thanksgiving — often seasonal in character.

The opening song is a gathering song, not a "traveling song." Its purpose is not to cover the time it takes the procession to arrive at the altar. Rather, its purpose is to offer members of the assembly  their first opportunity to open their hearts and voices in praise of God. The length of the song should be determined by the song itself. If the hymn has four stanzas and they are appropriate, then sing four stanzas. If the song has a trinitarian form, don't throw the Spirit out the window just because the presider gets to the altar first. If the song has twenty-four stanzas, sing four of the most appropriate stanzas. If the song is done well, it is an important energy that holds the assembly together and further binds individuals into community.

The beginning of the song or entrance music is the signal for the procession to begin, if there is to be a procession. In general, the procession goes like this: (There are possible variations.)

- One reader holding the lectionary leads the procession.
- Altar servers with cross and candles follow.
- The presider closes the procession.

Note: Other readers and eucharistic ministers do *not* walk in the procession. It is better that they sit with family friends toward the front of the church so that they can be readily available when they are needed.

All those in the procession walk to the altar at a dignified pace (neither too slow nor too fast). They make an appropriate and agreed-upon reverence to the altar (nod, bow, genuflection) and go to their respective places, as follows:

- Readers put the lectionary on the lectern.
- The presider goes to the presider's chair.
- Servers go to their places on the side.

The song continues until it is finished. Meanwhile the presider, who should be singing along with the assembly, arrives at his place and uses the final stanza or two of the song to establish his presence as leader of the assembly. This is an opportunity for him and for the assembly to join forces for the celebration they are about to begin.

On ordinary Sundays, I recommend that the procession be kept simple. Or you may choose the alternate procedure of no procession. If you follow more simple procedures on ordinary days, you make it possible to enlarge and enhance the procession on more festive occasions.

Gathering Song with No Procession. Here is an alternate possibility: Instead of having a procession, all the ministers take their respective places at the designated time. The presider begins the preparation period, as described above, and then turns over the time to the music leader. When the preparation has been accomplished, the music leader suggests that the entire assembly take a few moments of silence in preparation for the ritual beginning. If possible, a few seconds (forty or fifty) of improvised music can serve as background to this moment of quiet. At the time to begin, the music person gives a hand signal for all to rise and sing the opening song.

Every assembly should have one version of the Glory to God that it can belt out with all kinds of uninhibited energy whenever it gets to sing it.

Greeting and Penitential Rite.

When the opening song is concluded, the presider pauses a moment to gain the attention of the assembly. Then with the sign of the cross and a greeting, he continues to draw the assembly into this beginning of prayer and worship.

He immediately offers an appropriate introduction to the penitential rite in two or three carefully chosen sentences and invites the assembly to be silent. After a silence of some seconds, the deacon or another minister (leader, song leader) offers the petitions of the penitential rite. The presider closes the penitential rite with the usual formula. We should note that this formula is not an absolution and should not be accompanied with the sign of the cross.

Despite popular belief, the penitential rite is *not* a place for the presider to lead the congregation in an examination of sin. This is not the place for such an examination! Instead, it is far more appropriate to invoke the healing presence of God's love and then, in the petitions, praise the Lord for his constant intervention in our lives with his saving, merciful love. Here is an example, from the feast of the transfiguration of Jesus:

Presider: With Peter, James and John, we, too, are called to the mountain. With them, we cry out: 'Lord, It is good to be here!' Let us hold each other for a moment in the healing presence of our risen Lord.
Lord Jesus, we rejoice with you in your glory;
Lord, have mercy.

All: Lord, have mercy.

Presider: We hold the whole world up to your saving power;
Christ, have mercy.

All: Christ, have mercy.

Presider: We hold ourselves ready to help you transfigure the world we live in; Lord, have mercy.

All: Lord, have mercy.

Since the penitential rite holds an uneasy and tentative place in the overall pattern of the entrance rite, I suggest that normally you do not sing it. Singing it necessarily gives it a prominence it does not deserve. If we want to be faithful to the sign value of the rite, we will keep it moving. If you observe this pattern of economy, you will find that singing the penitential rite is far more effective during the time of Lent.

I also suggest that you use the rite of blessing with water much more frequently. It is entirely fitting as a beginning rite if the people understand that the rite is not a blessing with water, but a reminder of their baptism.

Glory to God. If this hymn is an assigned part of the entrance rite, it is now sung or spoken. The Glory to God is a hymn that finds an awkward place in this part of the Mass. It has squatter's rights because it has been there for centuries. But it is still an awkward intruder. At the present time the battle rages: Should it be sung, should it be spoken? The best response liturgically would be neither. Leave it out. Music people very often insist on singing it, no matter how good or how poor the melody. Since it is a hymn, they conclude we must sing it, just as we emphasize that

 responsorial psalm be sung because it is a song. This makes sense, but pastoral needs should take precedence. It is more important to achieve the overall ritual and sign value of the rite than to hold out for one part of that rite that has dubious value in serving the overall purpose. So I suggest compromise: Leave out the Glory to God whenever you can. Sing it on festive occasions if you have a version that is really worth singing and that involves the entire assembly at least in parts. Every assembly should have one version of the Glory to God that it can belt out with all kinds of uninhibited energy whenever it gets to sing it. One version is enough, if it is a good one.

A custom that is developing in this country is to use the Glory to God as a gathering song or as a song during the celebration of the rite of water blessing.

If you decide to recite the Glory to God, please do so in a lively and energetic fashion. No assembly should ever be left to attempt recitation on its own. The presider should lead the prayer. If he does not, the assembly will reduce it quickly and inevitably to its most monotonous common denominator.

Prayer of the Assembly. This prayer is really the opening prayer of the entire liturgy. If we had the ideal entrance rite (song, greeting and prayer) it would appear much more clearly as the opening prayer. As things are now, with the intrusion of the penitential rite and the Glory to God, this prayer comes off as being the conclusion of a series of devotional rites.

The presider can help rescue this prayer from its burial place by giving it careful attention. For instance, if he says "Let us pray," immediately and in a somewhat routine and casual manner, he gives off the signal that it is not very important. Instead, the presider can pause for a moment to get the attention of the assembly; then say intently: "Now let us pray together, first in silence."

The presider should then stand there for approximately thirty seconds in reflective silence. Only then does he look directly at the assembly and pray with and for them. Obviously he must have the sacramentary in such a position that he can do this. Too often a presider prays facing the book that is being held to the side. It is not the book that is important. It is the assembly that is important. Furthermore, the prayer is not the presider's prayer. It is the prayer of the assembly. The presider's task is not to read the prayer *for* the assembly, but to engage the attention of the assembly and to pray it *with* them. The presider should encourage the assembly to listen intently to the prayer and enter into it. This is what makes the prayer fruitful.

After the prayer, the server returns the sacramentary to a nearby table or places it on the altar where it will be used next.

The presider should then stand there for approximately thirty seconds in reflective silence.

The Individual Ministers

In addition to the primary liturgical minister, the church or the assembly, there are other ministers — presider, readers, music ministers, eucharistic ministers, servers, ushers, artists, etc. — are nec-

essary to help the celebrating assembly do its job. The specific con-
tribution of each individual ministry is unique and valuable. All
these individual ministers, however, must first understand themselves as members of the celebrating assembly. They too must be
filled with the sense of hospitality and with a desire to help make it
happen. When they have this sense, the individual ministers move
from isolation to full team membership. They are set free to minister to the community and to let the community minister to them.

The following are ten principles — I hesitate to call them rules
of thumb — for individual liturgical ministers. These principles
form the basis of a nonverbal "contract" between the celebrating
assembly and the individual ministers.

Principle 1: We Are Members of the Assembly. Individual ministers go out of their way to give clear signs of this important
awareness. They do this by listening deliberately to God's word, by
paying attention both to the needs of the assembly and to the flow
of the celebration and by joining wholeheartedly in song and prayer.

*Principle 2: Effective ministers give life to the as-
sembly; ineffective ministers deprive the assembly of
life.* When ministers are intent upon "doing their own thing"
rather than giving life to the assembly, they disrupt and harm the
celebration. For example, ushers who wander up and down the
aisle trying to seat latecomers during the proclamation of God's
word seriously interfere with the listening of the assembly. Likewise, music ministers who are busy getting music ready during
the readings seriously disturb the proclamation and give a sign
that they are not part of what is happening.

*Principle 3: Individual liturgical ministry is al-
ways a matter of service, never a matter of status or*

privilege. Individual liturgical ministers are not "better than" other members of the assembly. Individual ministers are "special" only in the sense that they have offered to share themselves and their "specialized" talents with the assembly, and this offer has been graciously accepted.

Principle 4: Ministry is a dialogue, a two-way communication. Individual ministers do not simply perform a role; they also make themselves present to others and share themselves with others. Readers share God's word and themselves with members of the assembly. Members of the assembly sing and pray together and share themselves with each other and with individual ministers. Eucharistic ministers share the body and blood of Jesus and themselves with other people. And so on.

Principle 5: Individual ministers are competent in the skills of their ministry. Individual ministers are willing to do their homework, to work with other ministers and to practice. They work to discover what they are doing and why they are doing it.

Principle 6: Effective ministers work as a team with other ministers to help give the celebration shape and dynamic. Teamwork among ministers is what ultimately makes the celebration powerful and moving. Genuine teamwork demands a great amount of communication, patience, hard work and generosity. It asks for being on time, reliability and the willingness to take an active part in training or renewal sessions for ministry.

Principle 7: Effective ministers deliberately put out energy. Effective ministers give life to the celebration when they wholeheartedly put themselves into communicating with others. They manifest this life-giving energy through posture, gestures, facial expressions and tone of speech.

Effective ministers give life to the assembly; ineffective ministers deprive the assembly of life.

Principle 8: Each person exercises only one ministry at a particular celebration. This principle allows each minister to give full time and attention to the ministry. It also invites more parish members to be engaged in different roles involved in the celebration.

Principle 9: All ministers are accountable to the parish community. A specific term of ministry (one, two or three years) makes its easier to negotiate conditions and expectations of service. It is not unreasonable to expect individual ministers to seek continuing education or to be recommissioned periodically.

Principle 10: Each minister is a person of faith and prayer. Those ministers who give themselves wholeheartedly to their ministry discover it to be a very important source of faith and prayer for themselves and for others. They pray about their ministry privately and with each other. They do their ministry with a deep sense of faith and commitment. Their manner not only conveys this message but encourages and supports the faith of others.

In addition to these ten principles, I would like to say a few words about specific individual ministries.

PRESIDER

The presider is first a member of the celebrating assembly, then the leader of the assembly and the leader of a team of ministers. We must understand these three roles very clearly.

Member of the Celebrating Assembly. The effective presider comes across first of all as an equal member of the assembly. With the assembly, the presider shares the responsibility to create the climate of Christian hospitality. Life-giving presiders make their identification with the assembly very clear by the manner of their personal presence. On the other hand, ineffective presiders set up a distance between themselves and the people.

Leader of the Assembly. Effective presiders lead the entire assembly in prayer, engaging people's attention and inviting dialogue. As leader, a good presider becomes an important catalyst for the liveliness of the celebration. No one can substitute for this role.

Leader of a Team of Ministers. Effective presiders recognize and respect the other ministerial roles (assembly, readers, music ministers, servers, communion ministers, ushers, artists, etc.) that are essential for making a good celebration. They go out of their way to make sure that each of these ministries becomes fully expressed and realized. At those times when other ministers are leading, the presider gracefully accepts — along with the entire assembly — the role of listening, singing, meditating and paying attention.

READERS

The ministry of the reader is a "people ministry," not a clergy

*The most
effective sign of a
good reader
is a person reading
with life, energy,
intelligence and
enthusiasm.*

ministry. Readers are not the presider's helpers; their ministry is rooted in their baptism. The most effective sign of a good reader is a person reading with life, energy, intelligence and enthusiasm. The skill of reading well is one of the more difficult skills, much more difficult than the skill of speaking. It calls for competent instruction. A priority, therefore, for every parish is to produce effective readers of the word. This means that a parish must have an ongoing program of preparation, practice and critique for its readers.

No instruction on paper can alone produce competent and interesting readers. Learning by doing is the only way. All I can do here is make some suggestions that I think can enhance the reading ministry.

- Readers must read with a great deal of energy — far, far more energy than they are accustomed to or even think appropriate.
- Readers who really want to be effective will try to incorporate everything that was said about cadence in the previous section for presiders.
- Effective readers — like good singers — learn to read from their stomach, not from their neck. They read with the kind of energy that can be felt in the body.
- Readers aim the reading to the very back wall of the church. (I have discovered that, as soon as you get readers to read with greater energy and to aim at the far back wall, there is immediate improvement in all other areas that make reading effective: diction, cadence, meaning, and so forth.)
- Good readers always distinguish between narrative and dialogue. They mark the difference with quality of voice, pace and deliberation.

- Good readers do not try to make the microphone do work they themselves should be doing. A microphone picks up and carries farther only what the reader puts in. (If there are pphtt-pphtt's in your reading, you are using the microphone badly. The best use is to back off, forget the microphone, read out to the assembly as if the microphone is not there, and let the sound system do its own work.)
- Good readers are not afraid to be enthusiastic, to become personally involved in what they are reading. (If you have a good story to read, read it enthusiastically. Read it as you would tell it.)

Attention to these details helps very much to create a climate and context that attracts people to listen. And that is what the ministry of reading is all about. The entire purpose is to engage people in the profound mystery of the living word being spoken and heard. The service of the word is not a time for learning a scripture lesson. It is time to experience the life-giving word of God made alive in the sound of the human word.

SERVERS

We have a longtime custom in the church of having young people act as servers. The role of server, as recently described by the church, is not one of "serving" at the eucharist. Instead, the server's primary role is to help prepare the worship service, lead the people in prayer and assist as a minister of communion. Because of this new emphasis, I believe we should open up this ministry to adult men and women. In making this suggestion I risk the wrath of some parents who want to see their little ones "serving at the altar." But I have decided to push for adult servers for the greater good of the entire assembly.

The server's primary role is to help prepare the worship service, lead the people in prayer and assist as a minister of communion.

In any event, whether adult people or little people fill the present role of server, here are some suggestions that could help reduce the clutter in the sanctuary and could make the role of server more effective.

- It is not compulsory for servers to wear any kind of distinctive robe. Whether men or women, girls or boys carry out the role of server, their garb should declare them to be "people" ministers, members of the assembly. This means that they might wear the kind of presentable clothes they ordinarily would wear to church. The protocol of good manners and good taste should always prevail and declare what is in order and out of order in the area of clothing.

- The best place for servers to sit might be with their families in church, not too far back, so that they can come up, perform their tasks when it is time and then return to their places. (Sometimes a presider schedules several servers as a kind of entourage for himself. It seems, however, that the presider seated alone is a stronger sign of leadership.) If this preferred arrangement is not workable, then have the servers sit off to the side of the sanctuary facing across and not straight out to the people. Their place, when they are not working, should be inconspicuous.

Pastoral musicians need to be competent.

These suggestions help toward a more effective celebration today and also look to the future. I suggest that you think about them and begin to work out a pastorally-sensitive pattern to implement them over a period of time in your parish.

MUSIC MINISTERS

"Music minister" is a generic term I use to designate all those who make music for worship: the choir director, organist, pianist, electronic keyboard player, cantor, song leader, choir members, guitarists, other singers, instrumentalists and ensembles. Basically all these pastoral musicians need to be competent in their art, skilled in their understanding and sense of the liturgy and able in some way to model and inspire Christian faith. These qualities apply to all ministers of music for liturgical celebration. Obviously they apply in greater measure to the person who is in charge and therefore finally responsible for what happens in the ministry of music.

"Music minister" is a generic term I use to designate all those who make music for worship: the choir director, organist, pianist, electronic keyboard player, cantor, song leader, choir members, guitarists, other singers, instrumentalists and ensembles.

EUCHARISTIC MINISTERS

Eucharistic ministers share the bread and cup *and themselves* with each person who approaches them. Their ministry is one of hospitable, personal presence in service to the celebrating assembly. Correspondingly, there should be enough ministers of communion appointed in a parish so that the ministry is no great burden to a few. A rule of thumb is that there should be enough ministers of communion so that they can serve at the eucharist they would ordinarily attend.

As is true for other ministers, the entire celebrating team should know beforehand who the ministers of communion are for that celebration. There also should be a way to

The experience of giving and receiving communion can become a rare moment of the experience of God.

know beforehand that they are present. One simple method is to have them arrive fifteen minutes ahead of time and sign or initial a list already prepared. The list may be in the sacristy or other convenient location. If this kind of practice is used for all ministers of a given eucharist, much potential confusion can be avoided in those last minutes before beginning. If any of the ministers do not show up by five minutes before the liturgy, they would not expect to serve. At that time the person in charge gets a substitute.

Eucharistic ministers share the bread and cup and themselves with each person who approaches them. Their ministry is one of hospitable, personal presence.

Effective eucharistic ministers work hard to make the moment of communion an experience of full personal presence. Remember, sacraments are not things. They are the personal actions of all who celebrate. The minister with bread in hand looks directly at the person receiving and says "The Body of Christ" in such a way that they together can share the moment as a living experience of presence in the simple but profound act of giving and receiving food. The minister holds the bread in such a way that the person who comes feels comfortable receiving either on the tongue or in the hand. The experience of giving and receiving communion can become a rare moment of the experience of God. Eucharistic ministers have a great deal to do with creating this moment by bringing their full presence to all the persons who come. The custom of saying the person's name, if you know it, adds to the personal quality of the moment and to the religious experience.

LEADER

There is still room for the role of leader at the eucharist. The leader (much like an head usher) makes the formal introductions at the beginning of the eucharist, leads some of the prayers, makes announcements, and so forth. The role is what remains of the original role of commentator. (Commentators are not needed today. Originally, when the liturgy was first undergoing change, they had the purpose of teaching.)

The leader should function at a place other than the lectern from which scripture is read. This lectern should not be used for any other purpose. The place for the leader should be adequate but simple; a stand with a microphone will do. The leader should be at his or her place only when actually functioning. At all other times the leader occupies a place convenient to the microphone, but off to the side. (Because the leader does have a role several times during the eucharist, it would be awkward if the seating were at a great distance from the stand and microphone.)

The primary task of the leader is to make the formal introduction of the celebration after all preparations have been completed and the celebrating assembly is ready to begin.

Other effective tasks for the leader include leading the petitions of the penitential rite, reading the verses of the responsorial psalm (if they are not sung), leading the creed, giving titles and pages for songs (only when truly necessary) and making the announcements.

Although much more could be said about each of the individual ministries, that is enough for now. What is important to re-

Many parishes lead off their entrance rite with a rather lengthy statement of theme. . . . a waste of time. It is the beginning of verbal overkill.

member is that all members of the celebrating assembly minister to one another. Individual ministers are, first and foremost, members of the celebrating assembly. Now it is time to explore in detail the ministry of pastoral music.

Proclaiming God's Love

IN SONG

The Assembly Gathers

Ministry of Hospitality . . . .
Spending time . . . . . .
Taking the trouble . . . .
Giving attention to others . . .
Attending to sacramental action . .
Being personally present . . .

The Assembly Listens

Ministry of the Word . . . .
Reading . . . . . .
Listening . . . . . .
Acclaiming . . . . .
Singing . . . . . .
Sharing silence . . . . .

The Assembly Responds

Ministry of Celebrating Eucharist . .
Remembering . . . . .
Giving thanks . . . . .
Invoking the Holy Spirit . . . .
Blessing . . . . . .
Praying . . . . . .
Reconciling . . . . .
Uniting with God and neighbor . .

The Assembly Goes Forth

Ministry of Discipleship . . . .
Proclaiming the good news . . .
Serving brothers, sisters and others .
Hungering for God

PRESENCE

. . . . . . At home, play and work
. . . . . . Introductory rites
. . . . . . Gathering (and song)
. . . . . . Sunday sprinkling
. . . . Glory to God
. . . . Opening prayer

WORD

. . . . . First Reading — silence
. . . . . Responsorial Psalm (sung)
. . . . . Second Reading — silence
. . . . Gospel Acclamation (sung)
. . . . . Gospel Proclamation
. . . . Homily, Creed, Intercessions

EUCHARIST

. . . . . Interlude (preparation)
. . . . . . Eucharistic Prayer
. . . . . . Sung acclamations
. . . . Communion Rite
. . . . . . Lord's Prayer
. . . . . . Sign of Peace
. . . . . Breaking of Bread
. . . Communion (with song and prayer)

MISSION

. . . . Concluding Rite
. . . . Blessing
. . . . Dismissal

Music ministers . . . must be aware how powerfully their efforts draw members of the assembly into the liturgical action.

Ministers of Pastoral Music

We are Christians because through the Christian community we have met Jesus Christ, heard his word in invitation, and responded to him in faith. We gather at Mass that we may hear and express our faith again in this assembly and, by expressing it, renew and deepen it.

We do not come to meet Christ as if he were absent from the rest of our lives.

General Notions

We have lots of problems in the area of church music. It will be some time, if ever, before we work our way through them to some shared understandings. Music problems are like philosophy problems. They never go away because they have roots in glands and hormones, in differing personal and professional taste buds.

If we are to move creatively into the future of liturgical celebration, we have to understand where we came from and see clearly where we want to go. For me the key to understanding where we came from and where we are to go is in the notion of the celebrating community or assembly. In the development of church music in the past, there was not a real understanding of the assembly. Now there is such a notion, and it is central for understanding what the new forms of worship are all about. I should like to discuss some of the specifics of the problem as I have experienced it and then move on to establish some ground rules for growth in the future. I have no intention of writing a treatise, which has been done enough already. If my own prejudices show through, it is because they exist. I suppose I cherish some of them. Certainly I do not apologize for them. I never have been neutral, but I find out that I am more neutral than many. Maybe it is the mellowing of age.

I would like to discuss three concepts of church music:

- the inherited concept of "sacred music,"
- the inherited concept of church music as "servant" and
- our current understanding of the *celebrating community.*

I think it is important to focus on these areas, however briefly, before proceeding to the practical matters about music ministers and to the suggestions that may concretely help the celebrating community.

"SACRED MUSIC"

The old and outmoded concept of "sacred music" still prevails and regulates the music people judge proper for church. We are just beginning to work our way out of the impasse. First, the notion of sacred music says that there is a certain music

We come together to deepen our awareness of, and commitment to, the action of his Spirit in the whole of our lives at every moment. We come together to acknowledge the love of God poured out among us in the work of the Spirit, to stand in awe and praise.

We are celebrating when we involve ourselves meaningfully in the thoughts, words, songs, and gestures of the worshiping community — when everything we do is wholehearted and authentic for us — when we mean the words and want to do what is done.

People in love make signs of love, not only to express their love but also to deepen it. Love never expressed dies. Christians' love for Christ and for one another and Christians' faith in Christ and in one another must be expressed in the signs and symbols of celebration or they will die.

Celebrations need not fail, even on a particular Sunday when our feelings do not match the invitation of Christ and his Church to worship. Faith does not always permeate our feelings. But the signs and symbols of worship can give bodily expression to faith as we celebrate. Our own faith is stimulated. We become one with others whose faith is similarly expressed. We rise above our own feelings to respond to God in prayer.

Faith grows when it is well expressed in celebration. Good celebrations foster and nourish faith. Poor celebrations may weaken and destroy it.

To celebrate the liturgy means to do the action or perform the sign in such a way that its full meaning and impact shine forth in clear and compelling fashion. Since liturgical signs are vehicles of communication and instruments of faith, they must be simple and comprehensible. Since they are directed to fellow human beings, they must be humanly attractive. They must be meaningful and appealing to the body of worshipers or they will fail to stir up faith and people will fail to worship the Father.

The signs of celebration should be short, clear, and unencumbered by useless repetition; they should be "within the people's powers of comprehension, and normally should not require much explanation."

sound that is appropriate to church. The concept holds in the Protestant, Roman and Orthodox traditions. It is probably more deeply rooted in the east than in the west. It grows out of the notion that there is a real dichotomy, a real separation between sacred and secular, between temple and marketplace. When we go into church we must take off our shoes and leave behind as much of "the world" as possible.

The roots of this notion are deeply cultural, philosophical and theological, and we cannot work through all those questions here. My own feeling is that we always run into trouble when we overemphasize either side of this tension.

Our music traditions of the recent past come out of too great an emphasis on the sacred over the profane. We have suffered as a result. Those of you like myself who go back through several decades remember the valiant efforts of church and papal documents to say that chant and polyphony were the models of what church music should sound like. Only grudging nods were made to any other kind of music. These well meant but very narrow attempts produced the sterile church music of the late nineteenth and early twentieth centuries — often uninspired imitations of earlier forms.

Another reinforcement of this segregated sacred music idea is the notion, still prevailing to some degree, that the boy soprano is the soprano sound par excellence for church music. This is particularly true in the English tradition. I think the boy soprano sound is fine and I support the successful efforts of many to develop it. But I find no reason to claim it as a more valid church sound than mixed or female voices. It is all part of the vague but strong prejudice that accepts the "disembodied" sound as more "spiritual." Personally I think it is part of the Platonic idea that the height of religious piety is reached when the spirit triumphs over flesh and we all become angels. I find the notion fit for angels, but not for people. I find it unacceptable in a religion that centers on the incarnation of God in human flesh.

There are times and places for church music that is sacred, heavenly, spiritual, even ethereal. But this must not become the exclusive model for music for worship.

CHURCH MUSIC AS "SERVANT"

When I was growing up, I heard constantly that church music must be a servant of worship; how perfectly Gregorian chant fit the Latin texts; and how faithfully, but perhaps more faintly, polyphonic music preserved the text. It was true, no doubt about it, until we began to celebrate

If the signs need explanation to communicate faith, they will often be watched instead of celebrated.

In true celebration each sign or sacramental action will be invested with the personal and prayerful faith, care, attention, and enthusiasm of those who carry it out.

— *Music in Catholic Worship 1–9*

Music should assist the assembled believers to express and share the gift of faith that is within them and to nourish and strengthen their interior commitment of faith.

— *Music in Catholic Worship 23*

53

There has been a radical shift of focus for church music. This shift of focus recognizes the important role of the assembly in worship.

in our own language. Then we ran into trouble. It was then that I realized that the concept of music as servant to worship meant only one thing: servant to the text. Not a word was ever said about music being a servant to the worshiping community. As a matter of fact, this concept was almost nonexistent. It is indeed essential that music serve the text or, better, that there be a successful marriage between words and melody. The real question, not really asked until now, is this: How does music make it possible for the celebrating community to worship better?

CURRENT UNDERSTANDING OF THE CELEBRATING COMMUNITY

Nobody was asking the question of how music serves the worshiping community because for much of the entire history of the western church there had not been a real role for the people of the worshiping community. The "congregation" had nothing to do except to be present and have things done for them: celebrants celebrating, choirs singing, organ playing. Nothing more than attention to sights and sounds was really expected of the people.

The glorious inheritance of church music — chant, polyphony, baroque — was oriented entirely toward choir and in-

struments. As such it was not suited to a worship that focused on the gathered people as the center of worship. It did not suit a worship that saw music primarily as a servant to the celebrating community as well as a servant to the text. In no way does this mean that our musical inheritance from the past cannot or should not be used. Let it be said very clearly that one important function of ministry in worship today still is to make beautiful music to be listened to. Let it be said also just as clearly that one of the important *active* functions of the celebrating community is to *listen to* and be affected by beautiful music.

But there has been a radical shift of focus for church music. This shift of focus recognizes the important role of the assembly in worship. (See *Giving Life: Ministry of the Parish Sunday Assembly — Assembly Edition,* by Eugene A. Walsh, pages 15–20.) We must face it and be willing to deal with it. In my over thirty-five years of experience with church music, I never thought of "dumping" the musical inheritance of the past any more than I thought of ignoring the creative musical energy of the present. I was forced to think through the matter very carefully. I had to revise criteria, redistribute values. During all that time the only real limitations on my

The pastoral effectiveness of a celebration will be heightened if the texts of readings, prayers, and songs correspond as closely as possible to the needs, religious dispositions, and aptitude of the participants. . . . The music used should be within the competence of most of the worshipers. It should suit their age-level, cultural background, and level of faith.
— *Music in Catholic Worship 15*

use of the musical inheritance were time and resources, never opportunity. The bottom line is that assembly-centered worship needs assembly-centered music, and we must refocus to answer that need.

Qualities of Effective Pastoral Musicians

"Pastoral musician" or "music minister" is a generic term. I use it here to designate all those who make music for worship . . . the choir director, the organist, the cantor and song leader, choir members, guitarists, other singers or instrumental musicians. What I suggest as valuable qualities for the music minister applies to all these people. Obviously they apply in greater measure to the person who is in charge and therefore finally responsible for what happens in the ministry of music.

I may be belaboring the obvious in saying that music ministers should be assets, not liabilities, to the community. Some may think this is too blunt. But I still see so many parish communities completely stymied in worship because they are tied hopelessly to ministers of music who are basically liabilities. The tragedy is that nobody — pastor, liturgy committee or anyone else — seems to be aware that

Music ministers should be assets, not liabilities, to the community.

the situation is so bad. They seem to take it for granted that mediocrity or the tyranny of personal taste is all right.

Music ministers are problems rather than assets to the degree that they are incompetent musically. They are problems also to the degree that they are incompetent ministerially. It is quite possible that an excellent musician is a poor minister of music. There is a specific skill of ministry in church music that has nothing to do with music. Musicians can be problems to the degree that they personally are incapable of dealing with other people. It may be that they feel threatened and therefore are very defensive. Maybe they are musical snobs. We need to be quite honest at this level and realize that such problem persons cripple not only the music but the entire worshipping community. Often the only answer is that they must go. I would never hire musicians for church ministry unless they demonstrate the ability and cheerful willingness to meet the requirements that I list below. These requirements are minimal.

MUSICAL REQUIREMENTS OF PASTORAL MUSICIANS

Musical Competence. The ministers of music should exhibit a reasonable level of competent performance in their

area of interest. The judgment to be made here is a musical judgment, and competent musical people are the ones who should be consulted for such a judgment. By competence I mean adequate proficiency in the musical skills demanded by the job: to produce a good hymn, an effective acclamation, a decent accompaniment, a proper tempo. These are very basic levels of performance. Anything below this level is incompetence.

Often it is said that music professionals are the only answer to the question of musical competence. This would be true if two conditions were realized: first, that there were enough of them to go around and, second, that parishes were willing to pay a decent, living wage. That so many parishes do not value Sunday worship enough to pay decent money is a matter for considerable dismay. It shows how values can be turned upside down. There is one more condition: that the musically skilled professional bring to the task all the other requirements listed below (see **Ministerial Requirements** on pages 60-67). Often, the professional musician does not qualify as a minister of music and is not really interested in developing those qualities.

It becomes plain that it is unrealistic to dwell on engaging professional musicians as the normative solution to parishes'

> The musician's gift must be recognized as a valued part of the pastoral effort, and for which proper compensation must be made. Clergy and musicians should strive for mutual respect and cooperation in the achievement of their common goals.
>
> — *Liturgical Music Today 66*

needs. I have found a middle solution to the problem of musical competence that does not compromise the essential requirements of that ministry. We know that there are many nonprofessionals in music who have much to offer. They need to be sought out and paid adequately. But there are still many parishes which simply do not have access even to nonprofessional music enthusiasts. They do have access to people who are minimally competent, the ones whom we are calling a problem. The solution: the parish engages these available persons and immediately begins to provide musical education and ministerial formation for them. The parish provides the opportunity for such persons to study and work with a professional or teacher, and pays for it. The parish also provides the opportunity to attend the kinds of workshops that will open up insights into ministry. The parish can even provide instruments of proper quality for promising people who cannot otherwise afford them. The parish makes these offers and also demands them as conditions for hiring. I have seen remarkable increases of competence as a result of this approach.

Musical Openness. Music ministers open to all kinds and styles of music are an asset. Music ministers who are

We do a disservice to musical values . . . when we confuse the judgment of music with the judgment of musical style. Style and value are two distinct judgments. Good music of new styles is finding a happy home in celebrations of today. To chant and polyphony we have effectively added the chorale hymn, restored responsorial singing to some extent, and employed many styles of contemporary composition. Music in folk idiom is finding acceptance in eucharistic celebrations. We must judge value within each style.

In modern times the Church has consistently recognized and freely admitted the use of various styles of music as an aid to liturgical worship. Since the promulgation of the Constitution on the Liturgy and more especially since the introduction of vernacular languages into the liturgy, there has arisen a more pressing need for musical compositions in idioms that can be sung by the congregation and thus further communal participation.

— *Music in Catholic Worship 28*

Although all liturgical music should be good, not all good music is suitable to the liturgy.

— *Music in Catholic Worship 29*

closed to some forms or styles of music for worship and are insistent upon others are liabilities. In engaging music personnel I ask very bluntly where they stand on this matter of openness. I expect them to exhibit a reasonable degree of openness in the beginning. And I expect them to develop a greater level of openness.

MINISTERIAL REQUIREMENTS OF PASTORAL MUSICIANS

In addition to basic musical requirements, ministerial requirements are of equal importance. A musician does not automatically qualify as a minister of music.

General Requirements. I expect a pastoral musician to be liturgically aware, that is, knowledgeable about what worship is — certainly willing to learn. I expect clear evidence on two points: a willingness to learn current theology of worship and a willingness to put aside inherited prejudices about worship. I want to see a degree of curiosity and eagerness.

I expect music ministers to give evidence that they understand what it means that church music is in service to the celebrating community, that music is first of all designed and chosen to help the community come to an experience of God rather than to provide an aesthetic experience. I expect, therefore, that music ministers are able and willing to work with others as a team.

Most of the skills of a good pastoral musician can be developed, even though he or she may not believe it. Encouragement has a lot to do with it also. Once pastoral musician candidates are found, they should be full participants in the liturgy planning. Some will have far more talent than others for the planning part. All pastoral musicians should have a thorough understanding of basic liturgical principles as found in the *General Instruction of the Roman Missal, Music in Catholic Worship* and *Liturgical Music Today* (available from OCP). From these documents pastoral musicians learn about priorities, distinctions and alternatives for a musical liturgy and thus learn how to program music for worship. Programming goes far beyond picking four hymns and an acclamation. It includes things such as a sense for so starting things, like the acclamations, that they become an integral part of the ritual and not an awkward attempt simply to follow directions.

These qualifications for leadership in pastoral music seem frightening at first, but it is not really so hard to find people who measure up. A parish should not stop look-

The nature of the liturgy itself will help to determine what kind of music is called for, what parts are to be preferred for singing, and who is to sing them.
— *Music in Catholic Worship 30*

A well-trained choir adds beauty and solemnity to the liturgy and also assists and encourages the singing of the congregation.
— *Music in Catholic Worship 36*

The quality of joy and enthusiasm which music adds to community worship cannot be gained in any other way. It imparts a sense of unity to the congregation and sets the appropriate tone for a particular celebration.

— *Music in Catholic Worship* 23

To determine the value of a given musical element in a liturgical celebration a threefold judgment must be made: musical, liturgical, and pastoral.

— *Music in Catholic Worship* 25

Musical Judgment. Is the music technically, aesthetically, and expressively good? This judgment is basic and primary and should be made by competent musicians. Only artistically sound music will be effective in the long run.

— *Music in Catholic Worship* 26

Liturgical Judgment. The nature of the liturgy itself will help to determine what kind of music is called for, what parts are to be pre-

ing if a good candidate doesn't materialize after a note in the Sunday bulletin. Keep looking, keep asking, keep listening . . . and set up a good training program.

Any parish that comes to know itself as a celebrating community begins early to take over the responsibility of planning and directing its worship precisely to bring about this experience of God. The parish community gets its work done through the team efforts of its individual ministries — presider, liturgy committee, music ministers. The important point is that the music ministers have only a part say in what music is chosen for celebration and how it is programmed, even performed. We will expand upon this point of view shortly. For now it is simply important that music ministers can accept this principle and are willing to work with it.

Musical, Liturgical and Pastoral Judgment. Capable musicians may make only one judgment: the musical judgment that tries to determine the quality of the music as music. Less capable musicians often do not make even a qualified musical judgment since they can operate only from personal taste. Untutored personal taste provides dubious criteria at best.

Judgments other than the musical

judgment need to be made: a liturgical judgment and a pastoral judgment. These are just as important — more important, in fact, than the musical judgment.

The liturgical judgment seeks to determine whether the music is appropriate for the text, for its place in the celebration, for the persons doing it.

The pastoral judgment tries to determine the overall fitness of the music for these people in this place at this time. These judgments determine the effectiveness of music in worship. Music ministers should know, at least, that such judgments need to be made and that they can be made only in cooperation with other qualified persons.

A Story. My friend Elaine began with a small folk group in a large suburban parish. The group was composed of adults and teenagers. Even though they worked together at the same Sunday celebration, they hardly spoke to one another. Part of the communication problem was the fact that they could not find a common language for saying how they felt about the old and new church. They were working out of different theologies.

Nevertheless, over a period to two or three years, the group enlarged to include about twenty-five members. Under Elaine's

ferred for singing, and who is to sing them.
— *Music in Catholic Worship 30*

Pastoral Judgment. The pastoral judgment governs the use and function of every element of celebration. Ideally this judgment is made by the planning team or committee. It is the judgment that must be made in this particular situation, in these concrete circumstances. Does music in the celebration enable these people to express their faith, in this place, in this age, in this culture?
— *Music in Catholic Worship 39*

direction they began to gain genuine musical excellence and a healthy sense of ministry. Through attention to the discipline and ministry of music, they found themselves becoming a wonderfully caring community. As is always the case, community was the fruit, a byproduct, of the efforts they made to become a first-class group of musical ministers for parish worship. They developed a beautiful sense of service. They began to understand that they were not just doing good music but that they were using their music as a tool for giving life and spreading the gospel.

More wonderful things happened. Barriers began to crumble. Members of the group discovered a growing desire to care for each other. They found ways of nourishing each other. In their efforts to reach musical excellence as a group, they found themselves challenging each other to reach beyond the possible. They helped one another discover gifts they had not been aware of. They found themselves supported in developing these emerging gifts. Individuals realized that they could never have done this by themselves.

As a consequence they became more attentive to the other members of the group, more appreciative of their differences as well as their likenesses. They learned how to rejoice in the different talents of different people, rather than being envious and jealous. They became less competitive with each other. More and more they became aware that their real strength and the service they offered the parish came from them as a group rather than as individuals.

Other good things happened. They became more and more a caring group, looking to be of help to each other as needs showed up. If a member became sick or was absent for any reason the members of the group immediately made themselves available for whatever was needed. They kept in touch. They prepared food. They ran errands. In the event of greater difficulties, such as a death in the family, group members simply embraced the persons who were touched by this grief and moved to do anything that was important for helping.

All this happened naturally rather than by design. By their efforts to be genuine ministers of music they found themselves become better human beings, better Christians. The effect of this example was noted in the parish and became the spark for other groups to do the same. So the music group in the parish became, as a group, a life-giving and Spirit-giving energy for themselves and for the parish. They were doing spiritual things and leading

Through attention to the discipline and ministry of music, they found themselves becoming a wonderfully caring community.

spiritual lives without really being all that aware of it. I have a feeling that they would have been surprised to know that they were doing "spiritual stuff." As far as they were concerned they were doing what anyone would do to meet and respond to the simple human needs of other people.

Through their efforts of musical discipline and ministry — and the prayer that flowed naturally from these efforts — members of this group of music ministers became more and more conscious that they had experienced a marvelous *conversion.* They got to know themselves as a genuine Christian community. They loved it!

Elaine has been gone from them for several years now. Members of the group have remained together for a long time, making not only sound musical and liturgical but also sound pastoral judgments.

Some Practical Suggestions

The worst place for a choir is in a gallery at the back of the church. I hope that music ministers make every possible attempt to secure their location up front. Any objection that they are a distraction up front comes from a lack of information about the music ministry and worship. Music ministers are either leading the en-

The *proper placing* of the organ and choir according to the arrangement and acoustics of the church will facilitate celebration. Practically speaking, the choir must be near the director and the organ (both console

tire celebrating community in song and therefore should be attended to; or they are providing music to be listened to and should be listened to; or they are, like everyone else, paying attention to what is taking place in the celebration. The bottom line is this: The assembly needs to be led.

The best sign of the relationship of the music people to the rest of the assembly is gained when they are so arranged up front that they are truly felt to be part of the whole community and are not segregated against the rest of the community. They are a specialized part of the community, of course, but they fully belong. It is important that they know themselves that way and are known as such by the whole assembly. Their location should be a basic sign of this reality.

There is need for easy communication between song leader and people, song leader and organist, song leader and choir, song leader and presider. Such communication becomes possible when the music people are all together up front.

CONDUCT OF PASTORAL MUSICIANS

A few words are in order on the conduct of the musicians in front of the gathered assembly. Since they are so plainly in view, they have a responsibility to make

and sound). The choir ought to be able to perform without too much distraction; the acoustics ought to give a lively presence of sound in the choir area and allow both tone and word to reach the congregation with clarity. Visually it is desirable that the choir appear to be part of the worshiping community, yet a part which serves in a unique way.

— *Music in Catholic Worship 38*

At times the choir, within the congregation of the faithful and as part of it, will assume the role of leadership, while at other times it will retain its own distinctive ministry. This means that the choir will lead the people in sung prayer, by alternating or re-inforcing the sacred song of the congregation, or by enhancing it with the addition of a musical elaboration. At other times in the course of liturgical celebration the choir alone will sing works whose musical demands enlist and challenge its competence.

— *Music in Catholic Worship 36*

Readings from scripture are the heart of the liturgy of the word. The homily, responsorial psalms, profession of faith, and general intercessions develop and complete it. In the readings, God speaks to his people and nourishes their spirit; Christ is present through his word. The homily explains the readings. The chants and the profession of faith comprise the people's acceptance of God's Word. It is of primary

good signs to the celebrating community. By their own conduct they assist greatly in winning people over to proper attitudes during the Sunday eucharist. First of all, they must learn to think of themselves as members of the whole community, not a privileged group apart. In practice, this means they oblige themselves to all the attitudes, actions and postures of the whole community except when they are doing their own particular work of providing music for the celebration. Music ministers and ushers — both of them have specialized ministries — tend to exempt themselves from doing what the whole community is called upon to do. To the extent that they do exempt themselves, they harm the celebration.

For instance, their conduct during the liturgy of the word can make a big difference in sign value. In order to be a proper sign for everyone at this time, they need to exercise considerable discipline. They do best, for instance, to stand during the readings and be visibly attentive to the readings. They likewise should give themselves over to the quiet reflective silence after the readings like everybody else. This period of shared, communal silence is no time for fussing around with music books or instruments. It is no time for standing up and getting ready to sing.

Any alien movement by the music ministers tends to break down the reflective attitude of assembly members. Therefore, they should be standing alert with everything ready so that on signal they can start the music. The effect of this sign on the assembly is powerful. It is a further reminder to everyone of what the period of silence is all about.

The same holds true for their stance and presence during the eucharistic prayer: careful attention to the prayer combined with full readiness to lead the acclamations. By graciously submitting themselves in this way to the discipline of the entire celebrating community, the music ministers are able to keep alive the awareness of their double role: members of the celebrating assembly and music ministers to that assembly.

Music ministers need to give clear evidence that they really do understand their particular role in the liturgies of the word and eucharist. They need to make clear that this understanding will guide both their choice of material and the manner in which they will help the assembly sing and listen. They need to be willing to give up old patterns of singing at Mass and take on new ones. They need to choose and sing music for the sake of the assembly, not for their own sake or even just for

importance that the people hear God's message of love, digest it with the aid of psalms, silence, and the homily, and respond, involving themselves in the great covenant of love and redemption.

— *Music in Catholic Worship 45*

The eucharistic prayer, a prayer of thanksgiving and sanctification, is the center of the entire celebration. By an introductory dialogue the priest invites the people to lift their hearts to God in praise and thanks; he unites them with himself in the prayer he addresses in their name to the Father through Jesus Christ. The meaning of the prayer is that the whole congregation joins itself to Christ in acknowledging the works of God and in offering the sacrifice. As a statement of the faith of the local assembly it is affirmed and ratified by all those present through acclamations of faith: the first acclamation or Sanctus, the memorial acclamation, and the Great Amen.

— *Music in Catholic Worship 47*

the sake of "going by the book."

A fairly large part of the tyranny exercised in the music area is brought about by the whim and caprice by which some music ministers choose their music and by the manner in which they sing or play it. In some instances you get the impression that they do not have a clue about the real *ministry* of music. Good musicians they may be. Music ministers they are not. They seem to be in a world unto themselves.

It becomes clear that music ministers are on target when they are single-minded about having the assembly sing with energy and enthusiasm the songs they are supposed to sing. That is the first and most important task of the music ministers. That is their ministry. If they do not put their energies into that task, they are simply not doing their jobs.

Music ministers need to be willing to engage in the overall teamwork and choreography that govern the movements of ministers of the word during the proclamation of the word and of ministers of the eucharist during the liturgy of the eucharist. They must be aware how powerfully their efforts draw members of the assembly into the liturgical action.

Music ministers are on target when they are single-minded about having the assembly sing with energy and enthusiasm the songs they are supposed to sing.

Structure and Dynamic of Sunday Eucharist

Impact on Music

The structure of the eucharistic celebration has a strong influence on the choice of music for the celebration, and also on the performance of that music. The Sunday eucharist does have a structure and a dynamic. The structure of our weekly liturgy is a relationship of the more important to the less important.

Assuming the energy of hospitable gathering of the assembly, the entrance rite is only introductory to the first major part of the eucharist, the celebration of God's word. Its main function is to make a good beginning and to bring everybody quickly and with energy to the hearing of the word. The same is true for the preparation of the gifts which is introductory to

the eucharistic prayer of the community. The preparation is far less important than the eucharistic prayer itself.

These facts of the structure of the eucharist create a principle: What is important should look important and sound important. What is less important should look and sound less important. The music ministers should regularly take this principle into account for the selection and performance of music at the Sunday eucharist.

In addition to structure, there is also an identifiable dynamic, an identifiable rhythm, in the celebration of good worship. The basic dynamic can be called proclamation and response. Each part of the Sunday eucharist starts somewhere, moves to climax and then falls off. The music ministers can help very much in creating these dynamics if they are aware of them and sensitive to their demands. Considering the requirements of both structure and dynamic, the following suggestions about the different kinds of music used at the eucharist can be helpful.

ACCLAMATIONS

Acclamations by nature are short, strong, joyful shouts of praise and thanksgiving. They should be written in such a style and sung in that style. The main ac-

What is important should look important and sound important. What is less important should look and sound less important.

The acclamations are shouts of joy which arise from the whole assembly as forceful and meaningful assents to God's Word and Action. They are important because they make some of the most significant moments of the Mass (gospel, eucharistic prayer, Lord's Prayer) stand out. It is of their nature that they be rhythmically strong, melodically appealing, and affirmative. The people should know the acclamations by heart in order to sing them spontaneously. Some variety is recommended and even imperative. The challenge to the composer and people alike is one of variety without confusion.

— *Music in Catholic Worship 53*

Holy, Holy, Holy Lord. This is the people's acclamation of praise concluding the preface of the eucharistic prayer. We join the whole communion of saints in acclaiming the Lord.

— *Music in Catholic Worship 56*

clamations at eucharist are the gospel acclamation and the three eucharistic acclamations: Holy Holy, memorial acclamation and the doxology with its Amen. Acclamations should follow closely on the words that introduce them. There is nothing worse than for the presider to cry out in rising crescendo, "And so we join . . . in our hymn of endless praise!" . . . and there is . . . pause . . . uneasy silence and then a rushed set of thumping measures of organ or guitar introduction. And then, hours later, it seems, the people let out a whimper of song. Instead of an acclamation there is a soggy sound, but the moment was destroyed long before the song began. Usually, there need be no introduction to an acclamation. One chord will do. If there is an introduction, it should be played in a way that does not undermine the effect of the acclamation. The singing of Holy Holy should follow immediately upon the words of the preface. It is up to the music director to know this and to work at it until it flows smoothly.

There are different musical ways to do this. Begin the instrumental introduction as the presider moves into the final phrase of the preface. Start the introduction "under" the final words of the preface so that the Holy Holy can continue it without interruption. This can be done very well

74

with a little practice. Once the members of the assembly know what is expected of them, they tend to respond quite well. And they like the effect and tend to say so. They get to make a real acclamation.

Another way is for both song leader and guitarist or organist to begin instantly after the call and then bring the people in with them. Good musicians can do it this way. The minister begins and skillfully helps the people to join in immediately. People do it well once it has been explained to them. These same techniques apply to the other eucharistic acclamations. It may sound like a small detail, but it makes a great difference in the dynamic movement of the eucharistic action.

RESPONSES

When using psalms responsorially as after the first reading, some important considerations arise: How can this responsorial form best enhance the hearing of the readings? How can this particular responsorial psalm function as part of the whole dynamic of the liturgy of the word? Music ministers need to know that the most important overall intent in putting the liturgy of the word together is to create the kind of climate and context that invites listening and reflection. The overall design of this part of the service involves team-

Responsorial Psalm. This unique and very important song is the response to the first lesson. The new lectionary's determination to match the content of the psalms to the theme of the reading is reflected in its listing of 900 refrains. The liturgy of the Word comes more fully to life if between the first two readings a cantor sings the psalm and all sing the response. Since most groups cannot learn a new response every week, seasonal refrains are offered in the lectionary itself and in the *Simple Gradual.* Other psalms and refrains may also be used, including psalms arranged in responsorial form and metrical and similar versions of psalms, provided they are used in accordance with the principles of the *Simple Gradual* and are selected in harmony with the liturgical season, feast or occasion. . . . To facilitate reflection, there may be a brief period of silence between the first reading and the responsorial psalm.

— *Music in Catholic Worship 63*

work on the part of the people, readers, presider and music ministers.

The music ministers have the responsibility for ensuring that the proper amount of silence — some twenty to thirty seconds — is created after the reading. At the end of the period of silence the music ministers start the refrain of the response. It is sung once by the song leader, then repeated by the whole assembly. This pattern of repeating the first refrain should always prevail, especially if the psalm is new to the assembly. Singing a refrain only once is very frustrating if the assembly is hearing the psalm for the first time. Then either the cantor or choir do the psalm verses, or one of the music ministers speaks the verses over a background of continuing music. Such a procedure produces a very fine response. It is good also if the music ministers understand that they are free either to sing the psalm response indicated for the given Sunday or to replace it with another from the common texts or seasonal psalms in the lectionary. They may also do more or less of the psalm, as the occasion or length of reading requires. Ordinarily, it is better to do less rather than more.

HYMNS

We use hymns a lot, perhaps more than any other style of song and perhaps

too much. Hymns were the only songs we had to work with until the new rites began to take hold. We set up the "four hymn syndrome." Since then we have come to learn how to use hymns more effectively. This is a task for the music minister. Music ministers must conspire with the rest of the celebrating team to rid their church of the four hymn pattern. It is a bad pattern. It is also up to the music ministers to know where hymns are effective and where they are not. A growing awareness of how to use different kinds of songs for different reasons at different times of the eucharist leads me to make the following suggestions.

The best place for a solid "foursquare" hymn is at the beginning of the celebration. As the first ritual action of the whole gathering community, the opening hymn or "gathering song" should get careful attention. It should be chosen for its strength and for its appropriateness to the occasion. Praise hymns and seasonal hymns are always acceptable, and there is a large repertoire to choose from. The hymn form calls for a clear, solid introduction that leads people to an expectation of singing. It should be determined beforehand just how many stanzas will be sung. There should be no surprises. Well informed, the presider gets time to wait in the presiding

> The two processional chants — the entrance song and the communion song — are very important for creating and sustaining an awareness of community.
>
> — *Music in Catholic Worship 60*

place, singing with the whole community while preparing for the role of leadership. The length of the hymn is never determined by how long it takes the presider to arrive in place, coming to a crashing halt because he or she has arrived. The opening hymn is the first action of the celebrating community, their first act of praise. This is what most importantly determines the choice and singing of this hymn.

The purpose of the gathering song is to offer assembly members their first opportunity to open hearts and voices in praise of God. If the song has twenty-four stanzas, sing four stanzas.

Normally the other desirable place for a hymn would be at the end of the celebration. Recently, though, new expectations are being voiced about the nature of this song and its place in the structure of the eucharist. Liturgists have pointed out that the closing song comes "after" the liturgy and is not part of it like the gathering song. For this reason they urge variety. Some Sundays, do not sing a closing song at all. Instead, have good recessional music as the people go out. When a hymn is sung, it is being suggested that only one or two verses be sung, quite a departure from the cry a few years ago: "we shall stay and we shall sing every last verse of this hymn. And you will like it!" Good practice today is for the presider to begin the procession out at the end of the first verse, or even before. The priest and other ministers should be at the front door just about the time the hymn is finished.

While we are talking about hymns, we should look at the two other times in the celebration where hymns became customary. First there is the part now known as the preparation of the gifts. I would say it is best not to sing a hymn here, certainly not a hymn about bread and wine. Here are my reasons. This is a secondary part of the liturgy; it comes after the climax of the liturgy of the word and it is an introduction to the eucharistic action coming up. This brief period is best used as a time of some relaxation. In most parishes the collection is taken up during this time, and the gifts are brought to the altar. A growing practice is to have instrumental music, or a choral or solo performance during this entire period of preparation.

Since this period often stretches out in time because of the collection, presiders or the music ministers tend to get nervous and think that the people ought to be singing. However, this time is much more valuable for relaxing, listening and reflecting. The people can be encouraged to use it profitably. There can be music during this time. It could be music for the assem-

The recessional song has never been an official part of the rite; hence musicians are free to plan music which provides an appropriate closing to the liturgy. A song is one possible choice. However, if the people have sung a song after communion, it may be advisable to use only an instrumental or choir recessional.

— *Music in Catholic Worship 73*

[A] song may accompany the procession and preparation of the gifts. It is not always necessary or desirable. Organ or instrumental music is also fitting at the time. When song is used, it need not speak of bread and wine or of offering. The proper function of this song is to accompany and celebrate the communal aspects of the procession. The text, therefore, can be any appropriate song of praise or of rejoicing in keeping with the season. The antiphons of the Roman Gradual, not included in the new Roman Missal, may be used with psalm verses. Instrumental interludes can effectively accompany the procession and preparation of the gifts and thus keep this part of the Mass in proper perspective relative to the eucharistic prayer which follows.

— *Music in Catholic Worship 71*

The communion song should foster a sense of unity. It should be simple and not demand great effort. It gives expression to the joy of unity in the body of Christ and the fulfillment of the mystery being celebrated. Because they emphasize adoration rather than communion, most benediction hymns are not suitable. . . . It is preferable that most songs used at the communion be seasonal in nature. . . . Topical songs may be used during the communion procession, provided these texts do not conflict with the paschal character of every Sunday.

— *Music in Catholic Worship 62*

bly to listen to. The music should start immediately after the Amen of the petition prayer and should continue without interruption until the presider gives the invitation to pray together. Music done in this manner makes a bridge from the beginning of this rite to its end, which helps the dynamic of proclamation and response to take over. I do not think the music should stop so that the priest can say the preparation prayers aloud.

We are moving to the practice of singing songs with repeated refrains at the time of Communion. The choir or song leader assumes the task of doing the verses, and the people sing only the refrain. I recommend this practice. It is not fitting for the people to have to sing all the time during Communion. Break it up. Have some silence. Have the choir sing something. Have the organist play something.

Since we are talking about Communion time, we might as well finish up with a suggestion about what is called the "communion meditation." It is still a problem. However, the time after Communion always has a reflective and meditative character. All choices of music should follow on that awareness. The meaning, mood, character and performance of the song should reinforce the meditative quality of the moment. It is not a time for a

showpiece. The ministerial role of the music persons is to help members of the assembly get in touch with themselves and with God, not with music as such. Music ministers also should understand that silence during this time is also a good option from time to time.

I have a rule of thumb for determining how much song to program at this time of the service. It grows out of the general principle that *it is better to sing less than more.* There's too much singing. If you have a few communion songs and a meditation song plus a closing song, you are crowding a lot of singing into a short space of time. Good programming calls for relieving this situation. If I have a communion song and a meditation song, then I usually do not sing a closing song. If I do not have a meditation song, I will be much more inclined to sing a closing song.

ORDINARY CHANTS

"Ordinary chants" refer to what used to be called the *order* of the Mass: *Kyrie, Gloria, Sanctus, Credo, Benedictus, Agnus Dei.* First, we must understand that the old division of "ordinary" and the "proper" of the eucharist is no longer a valid criterion for choosing what music is to be sung. We see that each of these ordinary chants is different because

Ordinary Chants . . . may be treated as individual choices. One or more may be sung; the others spoken.
— *Music in Catholic Worship 64*

This ancient hymn of praise . . . . may be introduced by celebrant, cantor, or choir. The restricted use of the Gloria, i.e., only on Sundays outside Advent and Lent and on solemnities and feasts, emphasizes its special and solemn character.
— *Music in Catholic Worship 66*

Lord Have Mercy. This short litany was traditionally a prayer of praise to the risen Christ. He has been raised and made "Lord," and we beg him to show his loving kindness.
— *Music in Catholic Worship 65*

The Agnus Dei is a litany-song to accompany the breaking of the bread in preparation for communion. The invocation and response may be repeated as the action demands. The final response is always "grant us peace." Unlike the "Holy, Holy, Holy Lord," and the Lord's Prayer, the "Lamb of God" is not necessarily a song of the people. Hence it may be sung by the choir, though the people should generally make the response.
— *Music in Catholic Worship 68*

Introductory Rites. The parts preceding the liturgy

each has a different function.

The *Gloria* is a hymn. It finds an awkward place in the introductory rites of the Mass. It has squatter's rights though because it has been there for centuries. But it is still an intruder. At the present time the battle rages: should it be sung or should it be spoken? The best response liturgically would be, "Leave it out."

The recitation of the *Gloria* and *Credo* is perhaps the most boring of all recitals. Listen sometime and try not to fall asleep before it is over. It would not be possible to devise a better way to destroy both prayer and ritual.

The Holy Holy is an acclamation. The Lord Have Mercy and Lamb of God are litany chants. The specific character of each of these songs determines its use and the musical setting used. In all instances, careful choices must be made about singing any one of these songs.

Choosing music for the gathering (entrance) rite offers a good example. Since the community has already taken the trouble to gather in hospitable presence to each other, the rite should lead with some dispatch to the Liturgy of the Word. If you sing an opening hymn plus the Lord Have Mercy and the Glory to God, you are piling up a lot of singing in one place and frustrating the real intent of the opening rite. Music ministers who know what they are doing ask themselves exactly why they are using each of these ordinary chants and then make their choices accordingly. "Because we did it that way in the past" is not a good enough reason. Nor is it a good enough reason to say, "But the music is so beautiful."

The important question is this: Does the song contribute to the overall dynamic and flow of the celebration? Does it help the celebration achieve its purpose? If you ask these questions, you will discover that you sing these ordinary chants only when there is a specific reason to do so. Examples are the use of the Lord, Have Mercy to enhance the penitential quality of Lent, or reserving the Glory to God for festive occasions and seasons like Christmas. The Lamb of God is a litany to accompany the breaking of the bread, and music ministers should try to perform it accordingly. This takes coordination.

There also is a custom in some places of singing a song during the gesture of peace. I would suggest that singing both this song and the Lamb of God litany is too much. In the gesture of peace, the gestures of presence and reconciliation are important, not the song. A good practice would be to begin an extended instrumen-

of the word, namely, the entrance, greeting, penitential rite, Kyrie, Gloria, and opening prayer or collect, have the character of introduction and preparation. The purpose of these rites is to help the assembled people become a worshiping community and to prepare them for listening to God's Word and celebrating the Eucharist. Of these parts the entrance song and the opening prayer are primary.

— *Music in Catholic Worship 44*

tal introduction to the Lamb of God litany midway during the sign of peace.

I would offer a similar suggestion about singing the Lord's Prayer. I prefer to say it well than to sing it very often. Few musical settings really enhance this prayer. Further, we should recognize that this is perhaps the one spoken prayer known by heart among most who have been baptized. To impose a sung setting is to deprive some people of the one prayer they can share in confidently.

Throughout this section we have been talking about good "programming." There are two extremes: sing everything you possibly can, or sing almost nothing. Both are bad. To sing all possible options is bothersome and irritating. Selection of music is comparable to underscoring or highlighting while studying a book. If you underscore everything, you succeed in highlighting nothing. So the very nature of music ministry calls for careful choosing and careful programming. Music is chosen to enhance the celebration. The primary purpose of liturgical music is to minister to the needs of the gathered assembly. Good ministers will always know why they are using a particular song before they proceed to include it. They will grow in this art of music programming.

USE OF RECORDED MUSIC

Today we have access to fine musical recording technologies and to the whole world of our music inheritance performed with skill and artistry. Warning: The living ritual action of the celebrating community singing cannot and should not be replaced with recorded music. However, there are times and occasions when carefully chosen recorded music may be necessary, for instance, an aria or a chorus from Handel's *Messiah* as a second Communion selection . . . provided this could not be performed live.

Function of the Song Leader

In summary, I would like to offer a few thoughts on the proper attitude of the song leader. The song leader in turn represents all pastoral musicians. It seems one of the most important qualities of a proper attitude in the song leader is zeal. By *zeal* I do not mean nervous energy. I mean exactly what the Second Vatican Council meant: "Zeal for the promotion and restoration of the liturgy is rightly held to be a sign of the providential dispositions of God in our time, a movement of the Holy Spirit. . . . Today it is a distinguishing mark of the Church's life." And the goal of an attitude of zeal is "that this pastoral-liturgical ac-

There is an art to teaching a hymn, the art of economical use of time and of knowing when to stop.

tion may become even more vigorous in the Church." *(Constitution on the Sacred Liturgy 43)*

Zeal changes a routine Sunday service into a life-giving parish liturgical celebration. If you study the plan for the parish Sunday assembly on page 48 of this booklet, you will become aware of how music can bring to life the words of God and actions of the church. The song leader, by careful attention to the important ritual moments, can draw assembly members to that same attention. For example, if a song leader keeps brushing lint off her or his suit during the proclamation of the gospel, a definite signal is given to the assembly. But if the song leader listens and faces the proclaimer, a different impression is given. The song leader should model to assembly members the important actions of gathering, listening, responding and going forth.

All ten principles of effective individual ministers — see the first chapter of this booklet: membership in the assembly, service rather than privilege, communication, competence and so forth — apply with special force to the song leader and all pastoral musicians. Think how these ten principles affect the times and orders of the Sunday parish celebration: the liturgy of the word and the liturgy of the eucharist.

Reflect also on my booklet, *Celebration: Theology, Ministry and Practice,* pages 60–75, and see how you as a music minister can apply these principles to the entrance rite, liturgy of the word, preparation of the table and gifts, eucharistic prayer and communion rite.

When a song leader has zeal for good liturgy and applies these ten principles, a life-giving celebration results. All the song leader's skills, practices and great ideas will not contribute to a life-giving celebration if he or she does not have zeal for good liturgy and apply the principles of effective ministers. But when attitude and practice combine, something wonderful happens.

Finally, just a few suggestions on teaching the community to sing and helping them to sing. I find some really bad mistakes being made in this area. They occur regularly enough to deserve comment. The biggest mistake is simply that of overkill. Song leaders talk too much and sing too much in teaching a song. There is an art to teaching a hymn, the art of economical use of time and of knowing when to stop. Here are some general rules of thumb:

- Make sure the people have music in front of them, not just words. Musical notes, even for the most musically illiterate, make a big difference.

Cantor. While there is no place in the liturgy for display of virtuosity for its own sake, artistry is valued, and an individual singer can effectively lead the assembly, attractively proclaim the Word of God in the psalm sung between the readings and take his or her part in other responsorial singing. Provision should be made for at least one or two properly trained singers . . . . The singer will present some simpler musical settings, with the people taking part, and can lead and support the faithful as far as is needed. The presence of such a singer is desirable even in churches which have a choir, for those celebrations in which the choir cannot take part but which may fittingly be performed with some solemnity and therefore with singing. . . . A trained and competent cantor can perform an important ministry by leading the congregation in common sacred song and in responsorial singing.

— *Music in Catholic Worship 35*

- Never do a useless thing. Rehearsal time is not a time to go over and over a piece until it is perfect. Rehearsals should never take more than four minutes. Trust, even if the people are not singing with you, that they are listening and entering into the preparation of their role as assembly participants.

- Never start a learning period with a new song. Always begin with a song people know. Ask them to start singing it and, after about two lines, stop them. Tell them it sounds good but could sound much better if they would put more effort into it. Then start to sing again. The song will be better. Stop it immediately after a line or two. The purpose has been accomplished. You have broken the ice. The people know it. They are ready.

- Then introduce the new song. Without any extra talking, ask the people to say aloud the words of the first verse in order to get the feel of it. Then ask them to look at the music and hum along as you sing it. As soon as they start humming they are beginning to learn. When people hum they can still pay good attention to the leader's singing. They can hear her or him leading the song, which they cannot do if they are singing aloud. They are able to sense much better how they are doing in the learning process.

- After the humming, ask the people to sing the first verse through softly and listen at the same time to the leader. Then repeat the first verse again at a normal level of volume. Good song leaders are there when they need to be, but they also know their role; that role diminishes when the sound of the assembly takes off.

- Be there when needed to invite and support the people. Don't dominate the sound of the singing assembly with constant singing through the microphone. Song leading means knowing well the use of the microphone, another area where feedback comes from friends in all parts of the place of worship. When the leader's relation with the assembly is good, he or she is able to use the microphone to move into and out of the song, first picking up the people, then letting them carry it.

- Don't practice too much. If the hymn is good you may find that only one place needs attention. Isolate that spot and clean it up. Do not sing the whole hymn, or even a whole verse, over and over again in order to clear up one mistake. If this is a first time with a new hymn, I would leave it there.

- Don't talk too much. Use the time for actual singing. We learn to sing by singing, and by no other way. As you rehearse, listen to the response and judge whether the people show familiarity with the song. If they do, *stop* right there. Don't rehearse what people already know. It bores them. Quit while you are ahead.

- Don't expect it to be perfect the first time around. You know the people will be singing it for some time to come, and each singing is another learning opportunity.

- Develop in yourself a good manner of leading so the songs become an integral part of the worship and not simply the fulfillment of a direction to sing. Without this ability to move from the printed page and give songs a life of their own, the leader is not meeting the need. Do not use the St. Bernard approach, overwhelming people with humor enthusiasm or ego. Nor a "Hitler" approach: "All right. We're going to sing this, and we're going to sing it *well!*" Thus another important characteristic of a good leader: Bad manners and bad taste have no place in church.

By using this approach and process, you do not irritate or bore the people. They begin to realize that learning a new song can be a satisfying experience.

Many song leaders use too much energy and make too many gestures in leading songs. Subtlety would seem to be a good principle here. Members of a symphony or a chorus follow a conductor because that's how they have been trained, and the nuances of the music will be lost if they do not. Not so for ordinary people in church on Sunday. They do not know how to follow, though they do respond to gestures of invitation and encouragement. The techniques of leading a chorus are not good techniques for leading a celebrating community. You do not have to beat a huge one, two, three, four in the air with your hand. You do not have to make enormous arm gestures. They are useless and terribly distracting. For singing in church, people need a good beginning signal and some support as they go on. The support comes from good voice signals and good face signals, much more than from hand signals.

If you have a good organist who knows how to lead a song, then you let the organist carry the lead. The people are influenced more by what they hear than by what they see. A good leader works with the organist, provided that the organist knows what to do. Over a period of time,

Do it with
a touch of class!
Enjoy it!
And as you enjoy it . . .
Please inform your
face!

you communicate to the people what needs to happen: the tempo, the energy, the enthusiasm. If you do this well with some humor and patience, the people will cooperate. After a while they begin to gain a sense of how to sing a song competently, and they learn much faster.

A motto for all song leaders might go like this:

> Know *what* you are doing
> and *why* you are doing it.
> Put your whole self into it.
> Work with the team.
> Do it with a touch of class!
> *Enjoy it!*
> And as you enjoy it . . .
> *Please inform your face!*

Repertoire

An important task of the music minister is that of responsible repertoire building. A good music minister gets in contact with the better publishers of current church music, staying aware of the musical, liturgical and pastoral judgments to be made about any new repertoire. A good music minister studies critical reviews of new works and listens to the commentaries of respected professionals. In consultation with other leaders in your parish, you work at designing the reper-

The practical preparation for each liturgical celebration should be done in a spirit of cooperation by all parties concerned, under the guidance of the rector of the church, whether it be ritual, pastoral, or musical matters. In practice this ordinarily means an organized "planning team" or committee which meets regularly to achieve creative and coordinated worship and a good use of the liturgical and musical options of a flexible liturgy.

The power of a liturgical celebration to share faith

toire you see as good for this parish over, say, three years. How many hymns, how many responsorial refrains, how many communion song refrains? How many Holy Holy acclamations do we need over three years? How many Alleluias? How many memorial acclamations? You make good judgments and choices, program new music intelligently and help the people learn at a sane pace.

Wise music ministers will use the same acclamations for two or three months. There is no need to change. People prefer what they get to know by heart. When people can close their eyes and sing many of their songs, that is a good sign.

You can do the same for responsorial refrains: Advent refrains, lenten refrains and refrains during the rest of the year. There is no need during Advent to use some different responsorial psalm each week. Find one that is really good and use it all four Sundays. The people get to know it, taste it, love it and sing it well. Instead of changing the refrain each week, let the music ministers do the work of varying the psalm verses. The same is true for the rest of the year. The same is also true for hymns. If you learn a new hymn once a month and sing it long enough so that it becomes familiar, think of how many hymns the parish community can count as

will frequently depend upon its unity — a unity drawn from the liturgical feast or season or from the readings appointed in the lectionary as well as artistic unity flowing from the skillful and sensitive selection of options, music, and related arts. The sacred scriptures ought to be the source and inspiration of sound planning for it is of the very nature of celebration that people hear the saving words and works of the Lord and then respond in meaningful signs and symbols. Where the readings of the lectionary possess a thematic unity, the other elements ought to be so arranged as to constitute a setting for and response to the message of the Word.

— *Music in Catholic Worship*
10–11

its own in the space of three years.

The temptation to change a lot of music from Sunday to Sunday is an ever-present trap for music ministers. Resist. Make up a one-, two- or three-year plan and stick with it. You will help build a musically articulate celebrating community, and members will love it. Music ministers will see to it that each assembly learns enough acclamations and other short pieces to get it through the highs and lows of festivities without books or aids for years to come.

The goal is that good musical choices become the articulate music tradition of this parish community. A further responsibility is that parish music ministers should make it their business to keep track of the music tradition of these people in this parish. Methods and systems are available to assist this vital process.

One last point for music ministers: Without teamwork liturgy does not happen. In the business of liturgical celebration things quickly fall apart when people try to work alone. We watch helplessly sometimes because ministers will not or cannot work together as a team. Remember, you never work alone. You are part of a team.

> The music selected must express the prayer of those who celebrate, while at the same time guarding against the imposition of private meanings on public rites.
>
> — *Liturgical Music Today 12*

Conclusion

Editor's note: The call to worship at the funeral of Eugene Walsh was an a cappella rendition by Gerald Brown, S.S., of this Quaker hymn:

My life flows on in endless song
Above earth's lamentation.
I hear the real though far-off hymn
that hails a new creation.

No storm can shake my inmost calm,
while to that Rock I'm clinging.
Since Love is Lord of heaven and earth,
How can I keep from singing!